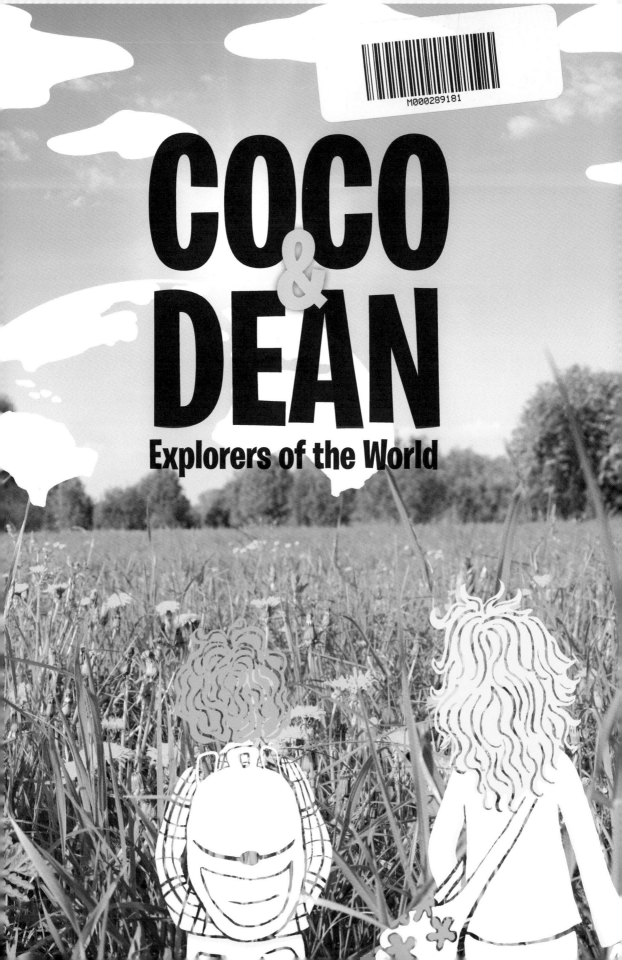

COCO & DEAN

Explorers of the World

Author Photo Courtesy of Nancy Evelyn

ISBN: 978-19-43258994

Library of Congress Control Number: 2015939294

Published by Warren Publishing, Inc.
Charlotte, NC
www.warrenpublishing.net
Printed in the United States

WP, Inc. is committed to improving environmental performance by driving down CO_2 emissions and reducing, reusing and recycling waste through their printing and delivery processes.

For Tom, Chloe, Dean, EE,
Poppy, Ommie and Boo
who nurture and share my
passionate environmental awareness.

COCO & DEAN

Explorers of the World

Contents

Think Like a Cardinal

The school bus slowed down as it approached Forest Drive. Big sister Chloe and her brother Dean stood up from their seats and got ready to move down the aisle and off the bus. This was their street. They hopped off the bus and immediately Dean said, "Race ya!"

Chloe said, "You know I could beat you, but not today. My left foot kind of hurts. I think I'm outgrowing my shoes again."

Dean sniped back at her, "Big Foot."

Chloe said, "I told you yesterday, don't call me that."

Dean got one more brotherly jab in before he listened to his sister. "Big Foot."

"Arrgghhh!" groaned Chloe.

In an attempt to ignore her brother, Chloe stared straight ahead and saw the repeating pattern of garbage cans and recycling cans on both sides of the street ahead of her. As she and Dean walked, she noticed stray pieces of waste strewn about the yards, like a bottle in the Jackson's yard, sheets of paper in the Gomez' yard, and more. They must have fallen out of the recycle bins, Chloe thought. "Yuck! Forest Drive looks more like a garbage dump than a forest," she expressed aloud.

"It looks more like your room!" Dean teased.

Just then, they watched a blazing red Cardinal land on the ground. It picked up something blue, and flew off again towards the woods behind the houses. "That can't be good," Chloe said.

Dean noticed the waste too, and began to pick up the pieces in his path and shoot them into the recycle bins like a game of basketball. "Dean has the ball, the other team is coming fast! Can he stand the pressure? He shoots! He scores!" he narrated.

At their house, Chloe and Dean ran inside to grab a snack and saw Mom's daily note with instructions for the afternoon. As Chloe took a bite of an apple, she read the note out loud. "Hi, kids. Hope you had a good day. I'll be home by 5:30. Before you play outside, please clean your rooms. And CoCo, feed your pets, too. Stay together outside!"

Dean finished his snack and said, "That's easy. My room's not so messy. Let's get outside in 10 minutes." Even though Dean was younger, he was the rule follower and organizer.

Chloe put her half-eaten apple on her dresser and thought, no way can I get this room clean in 10 minutes! The first thing she did was take off her tight shoes. Then she put some clothes away, but quickly became distracted by her pet tree frogs, and then said hello to Snowy, her soft, white bunny.

"Hi, Snowy! You sweet thing! Want to help me clean my room?" Chloe took Snowy out of her cage. While stacking up her craft supplies, something caught Chloe's eye outside. There at her window was another brilliant red Cardinal. "Hi! Are you the same bird from before? Are you playing with me?" And at that, the Cardinal flew towards the woods behind the house.

Dean popped his head through Chloe's door. "You ready?" As soon as the words were out of his mouth, he saw that she was not. "Come on, CoCo! My fort is calling me. Let's get this done." He began to help by quickly throwing all the dirty clothes into the basket, continuing his imaginary basketball game until he tripped over her shoes. "Ow! Do they make bigger shoes?"

"Ha ha! Very funny!" Chloe replied. "Thanks for finding my hiking shoes!"

"Hurry up!" Dean begged.

"Back in your cage, Snowy. See you in a little while." Chloe scrambled out of her room quickly, leaving the lights and radio on as she and Dean headed outside. "Let the adventure begin!" she shouted.

 Brother and sister took the well-trodden path behind their house into the woods. Dean dragged some scraps of wood for his fort. The beautiful scarlet Cardinal was on the top of their back gate. As they got closer, it zipped deeper into the woods.

"Today I'm adding the roof on my fort. You helping?" Dean asked Chloe.

"Not today. I think that Cardinal wants me to follow him. I'm headed this way," she said, pointing.

"You and your animal friends," Dean said, shaking his head. "Tell me what he says," he added sarcastically.

Following the Cardinal, Chloe was looking up and tromped right into a thick muddy puddle. SQUISH! Struggling to take another step, she quickly realized she was stuck. "Dean! Help!" she cried, but he didn't hear her. Tugging at her feet, she lost her balance and fell backward. SPLAT! Sitting on the ground looking around, she saw deer tracks, raccoon tracks (maybe – she wasn't sure about those) and bird tracks. She finally got her feet unstuck and couldn't help but notice the prints left behind. "My footprint is really huge! I mean, my feet aren't that large! Why are the animal tracks normal but mine look so big?" Chloe said aloud to herself, or so she thought.

Just then, the familiar crimson Cardinal swooped down, dropped to the ground beside her, and picked up a caterpillar with its beak. It flew up to its nest in the tree above. She looked at its tiny, proportionate footprints and said aloud, "What are you trying to tell me, Cardinal?" Chloe just knew the Cardinal was communicating with her, but what about? She climbed the neighboring tree, level with the bird's nest, and watched the Cardinal feed three babies. Nothing was wasted. As Chloe looked more closely, she saw something blue woven into the nest. "Is that the trash you picked up from the street? Interesting." Chloe watched the squawking birds and then scanned the horizon.

From her perch she could see the downtown towers in one direction and, in the other, her bedroom window with the light wastefully burning bright. "Oh, I didn't mean to leave that on." Her stomach growled and she remembered the half-eaten apple left on her dresser. Things were starting to click for Chloe.

Just then, Dean interrupted the moment. "CoCo, it's time for us to get home. Where are you?"

"Look up!" she responded.

"What are you doing up there? We've gotta go," he reminded her. Chloe relied on her brother to keep them both out of trouble!

"I think I just figured some things out!" Chloe said happily. Climbing down and then jumping to land next to her brother, she said, "My foot feels better. Race ya!" And she took off, beating Dean into the house.

Mom was home from work now and, as Chloe raced in, she said, "Hi, Mom. Be right back." Chloe ran upstairs and pulled out the paper and aluminum can from her garbage, setting them aside. Then she scooped up the shoes she'd outgrown and set them aside too. She turned off her radio and light and brought the items downstairs. The paper and can went in the recycle bin, while the shoes went in the give-away pile. Her mom noticed, but said nothing.

Supper was ready, and as Chloe began to fill her plate with a huge scoop of macaroni and cheese, she thought like the Cardinal and took a smaller helping. Chloe proceeded to clear her plate, wasting nothing. The whole family noticed.

Mom asked, "Would you like seconds, CoCo? I noticed you didn't take as much as usual."

"No thanks. I have all that I need." Chloe felt their eyes on her and grinned. "What? A little birdie told me I don't have to eat like a horse all the time."

"Finally! More for me!" cried Dean dramatically. "I'm a growing boy, you know!"

At bedtime, Chloe looked out the window. From there, she could see the woods behind her house and the downtown skyline in the distance. With her window open, she could hear an owl, frogs (including her own tree frogs), and also the buzz of cars on the highway. She thought about all the people on Forest Drive, at her school, and in her town, and remembered her teacher saying there are over 7 billion people in the world. Chloe realized

she'd learned a big lesson today from the Cardinal; one she couldn't keep to herself. Take only what we need and use what we take, Chloe thought. She started thinking about things she could do differently.

Dean popped his head in her room. "Night, CoCo."

"Night," she said. Her feet were casting a shadow on the wall, and even Dean noticed. "Hey, your feet look smaller."

"I think so, too."

"I'm still calling you Big Foot."

"Arrgghh! Good night, Dean." And then she said softly, "Thanks, Cardinal."

Explore with CoCo & Dean

- How did CoCo change from the beginning of the story to the end?

- What lesson did CoCo learn about the world?

- What did CoCo do to help our environment?

- So what about your footprint (a.k.a. impact)?! Everyone has one. That's right, over 7 billion people have an impact. What does that mean? Picture this:

  ° Every day there are well over 7 billion hits on the planet – demands for food, water, air, land, plants, animals, metals and minerals. Next, factor in the animals and the plants that need these same resources. Now imagine the waste created daily from 7 billion people and even more plants and animals. There is only so much the earth can support! Balancing what humans take with what nature can replace is a basic definition of environmental sustainability. DO NOT BE OVERWHELMED! Every positive action helps. This is known as the ripple effect. The sum of individual actions does benefit the earth – our home.

  ° Investigate your footprint, your country's footprint and how you can shrink it; there are many valid resources online. One recommendation is the Global Footprint Network. Take a few minutes to learn more about the ripple effect.

www.footprintnetwork.org

Conquering Rabbit Hill

Dean awoke ready for an adventure. He decided today was the day he would climb the mountain – the infamous mountain through the woods that had taunted him for weeks. You see, Dean and Chloe were spending time with their grandparents, and every day they explored the land around their home. Early in their stay, Dean discovered this mountain bursting high from the flat ground and he promised himself he'd climb it before the visit ended.

It was the last day of the visit with their grandparents, Ommie and Boo. Dean's parents surprised him by arriving before breakfast.

Dean could hear Ommie and Boo greeting his parents in the kitchen and saying the kids were still asleep.

"Good morning, early birds! It's nice to see you. I'll set two more places for breakfast!" said Ommie.

"Missing the kids, eh?" said Boo. "We've enjoyed having them around, and they've enjoyed it too. We might start calling them Lewis and Clark instead of CoCo and Dean! They've been all over this land."

In the room they shared, with twin beds on opposite walls, Dean whispered to Chloe, "CoCo, did you hear that? Mom and Dad are here. I can't leave yet!"

"Why not?" she yawned.

"I have to climb Rabbit Hill!" said Dean. He knew it was now or never, so he jumped out of bed and into his clothes and boots.

Chloe, sensing his urgency, pulled the pillow from over her head and asked, "You need help?"

"Come if you want, but hurry! I'm climbing Rabbit Hill before we leave today," he replied.

Dean attached a few supplies
to his trusty belt (rope,
water thermos, and gloves)
and ran through the kitchen
offering a quick hello to Ommie,
Boo, Mom and Dad as he filled his water bottle
and grabbed a biscuit. He was talking a mile a minute about where he was
off to and that he'd be back before lunch. He was out the door in seconds.

A minute later, Chloe came through the kitchen much more slowly, with
her hair a mess and her eyes still puffy from sleep. She hugged her mom
and dad. Then she took a sip of her dad's juice and grabbed a honey
biscuit off his plate. She gave him a playful kiss on the cheek and said,
"I'm going, too."

As she woke up, she began to move faster and eventually caught up with
her brother just as the path began to rise. They tromped through the
cold, briskly-flowing creek, and Chloe kicked the water so it splashed up
on Dean's back.

"CoCo!" said Dean.

"What!? Just trying to loosen you up. You're so serious this morning!"
said Chloe.

Then the trees cleared and there was Rabbit Hill. Dean pointed.

"Whoa," Chloe said. "It's bigger than I expected a rabbit hill to be."

Silence befell them as they began their ascent. In some places the climb
was like a steep hike, but in other places they had to take their time and
even use their hands to move higher. Along the way, Chloe noticed strange
objects poking through the brush. It caught her attention but she didn't
say anything about it. Finally, with a lot of effort and teamwork, they
reached the top of Rabbit Hill and Dean was elated. He high fived Chloe
and started running victory laps around the top cheering, "I did it! I did
it! I conquered Rabbit Hill!" On his third lap, he tripped. Chloe giggled.

Dean investigated. "Chloe, what is this?" he said, kicking at and then
pulling up a thick piece of black plastic buried in the dirt. More and more

was exposed – it seemed like it would never end. "CoCo, help me!" Dean grunted.

Brother and sister pulled with all their might as the dirt cracked and the black tarp was lifted. Partially buried underneath, they found a tire, a toy truck, a book, some fabric, a can and a plastic bag.

"Chloe, why is all this garbage in Rabbit Hill?" asked Dean.

"I don't know. This is definitely weird. Look at this!" she said, pulling up a toy car.

"Good grief! And here's a plastic bottle. It's like somebody used this mountain as their garbage can," Dean said with disgust. "I'm ready to go now." So, the two started their descent.

CoCo could see that her little brother was disappointed. She tried to cheer him up, saying, "You should be proud of yourself for climbing Rabbit Hill."

"You mean Garbage Hill?" he answered sarcastically. "Do you remember seeing that program about people living near landfills and picking through them for things they could use? I always thought that happened in other countries, but it's right here in Ommie and Boo's backyard. Do you think they know?"

They arrived back at the house, where Dean told his family the truth about Rabbit Hill. He looked at Ommie and Boo for answers. He could tell by their faces that they were not surprised by his discovery.

"I'm afraid Rabbit Hill is an old landfill – a place where garbage trucks bring trash," said Boo.

"You mean it's a mountain of trash? It isn't real?" asked Dean.

"Yes. Have you ever thought about where your trash goes?" asked Boo.

"No. I know the garbage truck picks it up from our house, but I never thought about it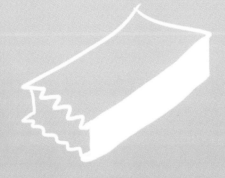

after that," said Dean. You could tell he was thinking about it now. "If this one is closed, then where is the trash going now?"

"Well, there are landfills all over the place and when one fills up, you have to start a new one," said Boo.

"But Boo, that's terrible to think of fake mountains all over the earth," said Dean.

"Well, if we throw stuff away, it's got to go somewhere. No one wants it in their backyard. Do you have another idea?" Boo pointed out.

"I guess that's why it's so important not to waste," said Dean.

"Yeah, and donating or recycling are other ways," Chloe chimed in.

"If we can reduce our waste, then we won't need as many fake mountains," said Dean.

"Sounds like you have a plan," she said.

"My wheels are turning. I sure don't want to see a landfill in our neighborhood." he said.

The entire drive home, Dean was texting his friends about the mountain of trash he'd just discovered.

"Are you glad you conquered Rabbit Hill?" asked Chloe.

"I climbed it, but I haven't conquered it yet," said Dean.

Explore with CoCo & Dean

- Think of something you have thrown away recently. Could it have been reused or upcycled?

- Pick several pieces of trash like a milk carton, a plastic bag, a toothbrush, etc. and brainstorm ways each item could be reused or upcycled.

- Do you know where your trash goes? Draw a map of the landfills, recycling centers and donation sites in your town.

- In Conquering Rabbit Hill, Dean mentions a story about people taking waste from landfills for their personal use. This is a true story of children in Paraguay finding discard from a landfill to make musical instruments. The children are inspired to reduce waste and reuse waste materials to make beautiful music. This story of upcycling is worth reading more about.

http://www.landfillharmonicmovie.com

Vacation Vortex

It was Wednesday, and Chloe and Dean had just arrived home from school. They went straight to the kitchen for a snack, and in the fruit bowl there were two envelopes – one labeled Dean, and the other, CoCo. Chloe and Dean looked at each other, then excitedly ripped their envelopes open. Inside each was a ticket and a note that read:

> School will be out in just seven days.
> Our summer will start in an unusual way.
> Get your bag packed. Bring a life jacket, too.
> We're spending a week on the ocean so blue.

Brother and sister were excited, but they still didn't know exactly what this meant, so they picked up the phone to call their parents at work. As the phone was ringing, Mom and Dad jumped out from around the corner and yelled, "Surprise!"

Mom said, "You've both worked so hard in school this year, and Dad and I have been so busy at work that we felt this whole family needed a vacation! So..."

"We're going on a cruise!" they said together. The whole family hugged, jumped and cheered. Now it was going to be especially hard for the kids to get through the last week of school.

After the shock wore off, the kids started asking questions about the trip like, "Where are we going?" and "What kind of boat?" They quickly learned this would be an amazing adventure.

Their dad showed them a map of the Hawaiian Islands and said, "This is where we start and this is where we stop. Where we go in between is up to you."

SCHOOL WILL BE OUT
7 DAYS
OUR SUMMER WILL STA
AN UNUSUAL WAY.
GET YOUR BAG PACKE
BRING A LIFE JACKET
WE'RE SPENDING A WE
THE OCEAN SO
Blue

Chloe and Dean's eyes got big. Chloe said, "Wow! This surprise keeps getting better and better! I'm going to find a beautiful island with exotic wildlife and interesting people."

Dean said, "I'm going to find a place with a volcano and a waterfall."

"We've got a sailboat," said Dad, "so we're free to chart our own course."

"I'm so excited," said Mom. "This is going to be a magnificent trip. The Pacific Ocean is so pristine. We are going to experience such beauty. Trust me, kids. You won't believe how beautiful everything is!"

The school year ended well for Chloe and Dean, with the usual tests and celebrations. Since there wasn't much homework the last week of school, each evening Chloe and Dean researched where their sailboat should go. Together they decided on the islands they would visit in Hawaii. Everything they could find about Hawaii made it sound and look more unique than any place they had ever been. They pitched the ideas to their parents, who wholeheartedly agreed.

Mom explained that the boat was small and they had to pack wisely. "Save room in your bag for this," she said, as she gave each child a journal. "I have a feeling your life will change on this trip and you just might be inspired to jot some things down."

SATURDAY

Starting their vacation was a journey in itself. They drove, flew, and drove again to their port on the East Coast of Hawaii. Once there, they met the captain and crew of the sailboat and discussed their route. They loaded their very limited luggage, laid claim to their very small bunks and explored every nook and cranny of the interesting sailboat. They were all very excited about the adventures that lay ahead.

At every stop along the journey, they would take time to get off the boat and explore the area. They enjoyed hikes along the mountainous coast, boogie boarding on the waves, snorkeling, and even a bike ride to an active volcano. This was Dean's favorite part. It was so cool to see the lava and feel the heat. It was amazing!

Chloe couldn't stop taking pictures of all the gorgeous flowers and birds she found during each excursion. Every one she saw was her new favorite!

Daily, Chloe and Dean helped catch fish for dinner – that was cool! The boat crew were skilled fishermen, and they taught the kids some new tricks. "We don't have fish like this in our pond!" exclaimed Chloe. "This is my kind of fishing!"

At night they were so exhausted that they didn't even miss the TV or Internet. In fact, they didn't even mind the teeny, tiny bunk beds. The coolest part was being rocked to sleep by the waters of the Pacific Ocean!

Three days and two islands into their vacation, Mom asked, "Have you two written in your journals yet?"

"Oh, I forgot about it," said Dean.

"I wrote down a couple of the new bird and flower names," said Chloe.

"Why don't you spend some time on that this morning?" encouraged Mom.

"I'm going to need a thesaurus to find new words for beautiful. Everything I see is simply beautiful. Now I know why they call it paradise," said Chloe.

"I agree. It's just magnificent to see this part of God's world," said Mom.

"I think I'll move here when I grow up," said Chloe.

"That sounds fine to me. Dad and I might follow you!" said Mom. "What about you, Dean?"

"Yo ho ho, a pirate's life for me..." sang Dean in his best pirate voice.

"I guess that means yes," chuckled Dad.

"We have just a couple of days left before we fly home. The captain was telling me about a helicopter excursion. Are you guys interested?" asked Dad.

"Yes!" replied Chloe and Dean in unison.

"Alright then, I guess that's settled! I'll make the reservation," Dad said.

The next morning came quickly. The whole family ate fish for breakfast and then jumped in the water with their snorkels. They were amazed at the beauty just beneath the water. Coral, plants, and fish of all colors, shapes, and sizes swam above the black lava rocks and tan sand. Dean was snapping pictures with his underwater camera.

The helicopter ride was next.

"I'm nervous," said Chloe.

"I'm not. I'm excited," said Dean. "This is going to be the coolest part of our trip!"

They boarded the helicopter and buckled in. Each had a window seat. The helicopter lifted and their stomachs jumped as though they were on a roller coaster. As the helicopter rose higher, the scenery was amazing: rugged, black and brown mountain peaks, perfectly blue (just as they imagined it!) water, jungle-like tree canopies and vegetation growing in patches around the island. There was silence between the siblings. What could they say?! They had to be thinking the same thing – what amazing, beautiful, indescribable sites! The chopper took them over the water and then up the coast of an island called Oahu. At one point, the pilot lowered the chopper and they could see a line of blue, yellow, red, and white stuff on the sand. The pilot spoke through the headsets and told them it was plastic trash washed up from the ocean.

She explained, "Where the ocean currents collide in this part of the Pacific (and in other oceans of the world), floating plastic trash collects like a barge of garbage. People have started calling it the Plastic Vortex. When the pieces break free from the force, some of them wash up on the shore like this."

Dean asked, "Why don't they clean it up?"

The pilot answered, "People do garbage pick-ups on the beach, but the plastic keeps coming, and some of it is so small it's hard to capture. Besides it being dirty and looking bad to humans, it looks like food to the marine life and, sadly, they gobble it up."

Chloe's eyes filled with tears, and when she spoke she sounded angry. "This is ridiculous. If more people could see this they would definitely do something about it."

Dean said to Chloe, "What can we do about it? It's not like it's our trash."

Chloe responded in a disgusted tone as she stared out the window. "Well, you don't know that. Some of your old toys could be floating right below us."

She paused and then said sarcastically, "Dean, look at that red thing. I think that's your old super hero shield."

"Hey, that's not cool. I would never throw my garbage into the ocean," said Dean.

"I know. This just makes me mad! Everything on our vacation has been so awesome and now we see this sad scene..." her voice trailed off.

The pilot spoke up, saying, "I show this to everyone, hoping it will spark a fire in someone's heart."

On the ride back, Chloe and Dean hardly talked. When they got back to the boat, Chloe grabbed the captain of the sailboat and asked that he take them all to the plastic beach. Chloe was somber the whole way. When they arrived, the trash was immediately visible.

The captain said, "This breaks my heart."

Chloe and Dean spent their last day of vacation picking up plastic trash of all shapes, sizes and colors. Some bits were unrecognizable and other pieces were obvious. Their parents and even the crew worked, too. After a while, Chloe smiled. It felt good to help and she knew she had to share this with her friends back home.

"Hey Dean, are you taking pictures of this?" she asked.

"No. I only wanted pictures of cool stuff to show my friends," he answered.

"I know what you mean, but I don't think people will believe us if we don't have proof. Will you please take a bunch of pictures? I have a plan," Chloe said.

Both of them realized that seeing is believing. Over the rest of the summer, they worked together to create a video of their trip showing the contrast of nature's beauty to the Plastic Vortex. They shared the video online and pretty soon accepted requests to speak to kids all over town – Girl Scouts, Boy Scouts, churches and camps. Chloe always started the conversation like this: "Did you know that sea monsters exist?" Let me tell you about one in the Pacific Ocean that eats plastic garbage!"

Explore with CoCo & Dean

- At the beginning of the story, CoCo and Dean found a poem. Can you write a four line poem about garbage and the ocean?

- If you don't live near an ocean or have never been to an ocean, it doesn't matter. You still need a healthy ocean!

- Why do you need a healthy ocean?
  - Oceans provide at least 50% of the oxygen in the air
  - Oceans contribute to our weather patterns
  - Oceans influence the temperature of Earth
  - Oceans provide food
  - Oceans provide jobs
  - Oceans provide places to live and play

- If this story moves you to action, The Ocean Conservancy has resources to keep trash out of our oceans. The Ocean Conservancy is a nonprofit organized in 1972 to protect the vitality of oceans.

www.oceanconservancy.org and search for '10 Things you can do for trash free seas'.

GLOSSARY

Cardinal — a North and South American songbird; males are red with an orange beak and black mask; females are tan with a few muted red feathers, an orange beak and a black mask

Ecological Footprint — the impact an individual has on its environment through daily living (eating, going places, making waste)

Environmental Sustainability — using resources in an amount that is equal to or less than the amount nature can produce

Garbage — material that is discarded

Landfill — a place designed to collect garbage; usually an extremely large pit is designed and trash is collected until a mountain is formed

Lava Rock — a type of rock formed when molten lava flows from a volcano or rift and hardens upon cooling

Overpopulation — when the number of a species is too great for the habitat and begins to deplete resources necessary for life

Plastic Vortex — areas in the oceans where floating plastic debris collects as a result of the colliding currents

Population — the number of a species within a given area

Recycling — incorporating a used product into a new product

Sustainability — maintaining something for a future generation

Upcycling — taking discarded material and finding a new use for it

Vortex — a swirling area in oceans where currents collide

About the Author

Photo Credit: Nancy Evelyn

Emily Scofield

An accomplished leader and educator, Emily Scofield focuses her career on environmental protection. She is currently the Executive Director of the U.S. Green Building Council – North Carolina Chapter and runs a consulting business, ESH Consulting, LLC. Drawing on more than 14 years of experience in environmental initiatives, she regularly communicates with politicians, civic leaders, corporate executives, interested citizens and students to promote sustainable communities. Emily educates on sustainability through various speaking engagements and in articles featured in numerous publications. 'CoCo and Dean: Explorers of the World' is the first in a series of adventure tales to elevate children's environmental awareness.

Emily has been recognized in the Charlotte Business Journal's 2012 40 Under 40 list recognizing business and civic leaders in the city under the age of 40. Additionally, the Hornets' Nest Girl Scout Council honored Emily with a 2012 Women of Distinction Award for Environmental Leadership. More recently, Emily has been honored with The University of Georgia's 40 Under 40 list recognizing accomplished alumni who represent the three pillars of UGA and in 2014 was named one of Charlotte's Top Women in Business.

Emily earned a Bachelors of Arts degree in Biology from Queens University of Charlotte and then earned a Master of Science in Environmental Health Science from the University of Georgia. Emily's family includes husband, Tom and children, Chloe and Dean. She is an active member of her church and community volunteer.